NASHVILLE CLASSICS

B♭ TENOR SAXOPHONE/TRUMPET

E♭ ALTO SAXOPHONE

To access audio visit:
www.halleonard.com/mylibrary

5010-4221-7338-8880

ISBN 978-1-59615-698-2

EXCLUSIVELY DISTRIBUTED BY

HAL•LEONARD®

7777 W. BLUEMOUND RD. P.O. BOX 13819 MILWAUKEE, WI 53213

© 2005, 2014 MMO Music Group, Inc.
All Rights Reserved

For all works contained herein:
Unauthorized copying, arranging, adapting, recording, Internet posting, public performance,
or other distribution of the printed or recorded music in this publication is an infringement of copyright.
Infringers are liable under the law.

Visit Hal Leonard Online at
www.halleonard.com

Boots Randolph

When Boots Randolph starts "tootin' his horn," he does more than just play the saxophone. More than just pop out music notes. And that's why his saxophone sounds like it can sing, can talk, can almost speak to deaf ears! His ability is awesome. His versatile style has no equal. And he's been bringing audiences to their feet ever since the early sixties, when his signature song, *Yakety Sax*, first hit the airwaves. It took off like gangbusters and turned the young musician into a celebrity, probably before some of his friends in the hills of Kentucky could have even spelled it!

A native of Paducah, Kentucky, Boots, whose real name is Homer Louis Randolph, grew up in the rural community of Cadiz. Young Homer was tagged with the nickname "Boots" by his brother, Bob, without dreaming it would one day be that of an international star! The Randolphs were always a creative clan, rich in musical talent, and their family band initially provided Boots with the first of his opportunities on stage. He learned to play a variety of instruments, but settled on the sax, at age 16. Years later, he was to make it his career choice, while working for Uncle Sam, during which time he was privileged to perform with the Army band. After his discharge in 1946, Boots Randolph began putting his "chops" to work professionally. However, it wasn't until 1961 that he moved to Music City, on the heels of his successful trademark tune or, as he tells it, "that song (*Yakety Sax*) is what took me out of the hills of Kentucky and put me in the hills of Tennessee!" The song gave him the prestige of being a hit artist. Almost instantly, the Sax Man was seriously being sought after as a studio musician, and he was soon picking saxophone on recording sessions for numerous stars.

Boots Randolph was the first to ever play sax on recordings with Elvis, and the only one to ever play solo with him, in addition to recording on the soundtracks for eight of his movies. Boots also played on such diverse recordings as Roy Orbison's *Oh, Pretty Woman*, Al Hirt's *Java*, REO Speedwagon's *Little Queenie*, and Brenda Lee's *Rockin' 'Round the Christmas Tree*. In fact, he has a 30-year history of playing on records with her, including *I Want to Be Wanted* and *I'm Sorry*. An array of other artists who have added the Yakety Sax touch to their recordings include Chet Atkins, Buddy Holly, Floyd Cramer, Alabama, Johnny Cash, Richie Cole, Pete Fountain, Tommy Newsom and Doc Severinsen.

His unique style of sax, coupled with tremendous popularity on Music City sessions in the sixties, automatically made Randolph a major player in creating the now famous "Nashville Sound." Without question, it was Randolph's particular blend of Dixieland jazz, along with some Swingin' honky-tonk, which helped Nashville music makers turn hillbilly records into a hybrid sound that literally transformed Nashville into the Country Music Capitol of the world! And to this day, Randolph still has more calls for his "Saxy" sound at studio sessions than he can handle. While most people only associate Randolph with his self-written, multi-million seller *Yakety Sax*, he also had other big hits in the form of gold (a half-million in sales) on *The Shadow of Your Smile* in 1966. Plus, he "hit gold" numerous other times through recordings made with others, including *Honey in the Horn*, *Java*, and *Cotton* by Al Hirt, not to mention the countless consecutive gold records by Elvis. He also has over 40 albums to his credit on the Monument label. Randolph spent 15 years touring with fellow instrumentalists Chet Atkins and Floyd Cramer. He's also taken his "Yakety Sax" to numerous network TV shows including the Ed Sullivan Show, Kraft Music Hall, The Tonight Show with Johnny Carson, Merv Griffin Show, Mike Douglas Show, Joey Bishop Show, Steve Lawrence Show, and the Boston Pops. He's made numerous TV appearances on TNN'S Music City Tonight and Prime Time Country.

After performing all across the country in some of the most posh clubs ever built, Boots Randolph took the plunge in 1977, borrowed half-a-million bucks to restore an historic building in Nashville Printer's Alley, and opened his own dinner club called Boots Randolph's. He performed there on a regular basis, and enjoyed a successful run with the club for 17 years, before he called it quits. When he closed the club, Randolph had vowed to "go fishing," but it was barely a year later in 1996, when he found himself back in business, pairing up with Danny Davis, as they embarked on a brand new venture in Nashville called The Stardust Theatre, featuring both artists in concert. Two years later, they each returned to their respective on-the-road schedules. Having headlined at almost every fair, jazz festival and convention in the country, as well as performing throughout Europe, definitely puts Boots Randolph in the category of being a saxophone player WITH EXPERIENCE!

Over the years, this legendary musician has written chapter after chapter of music history, forever etched in sound and to this day, he continues to entertain audiences with the same enthusiasm he's had since day one. Boots is his name. SAX is his game! His horn is a Selmer Super 80 Series II. He uses a Bobby Dukoff D-9 mouthpiece, and a #3 Rico reed.

Music Minus One is particularly pleased to be able to add Boots Randolph to the MMO family of fine musicians who have graced our catalogue. This illustrious saxophonist so intimately associated with country music has performed with every notable singer of that genre, Elvis, Orbison, Chet Atkins, Buddy Holly, Floyd Cramer, Johnny Cash, Alabama, the list seems endless. His pop music credentials include Brenda Lee, Al Hirt, Richie Cole, Pete Fountain, Tommy Newsom, Doc Severinsen, his greatness has touched greatness.

CONTENTS

Bb Instrument

Crazy

Willie Nelson

Tenor Sax
(or Bb Trumpet)

©Sony/ATV Songs (BMI). All rights reserved.
International Copyright Secured. Used by permission.

Bb Instrument

You Don't Know Me

Eddy Arnold/Cindy Walker

Tenor Sax
(or Bb Trumpet)

©Unichappel Music Inc. (BMI). All rights reserved.
International Copyright Secured. Used by permission.

Last Date

One measure of taps precedes music

Floyd Cramer

©Acuff Rose Music Inc. (BMI). All rights reserved.
International Copyright Secured. Used by permission.

Night Life

Breeland/Nelson/Buskirk

©Glad Music (BMI)/Sony ATV Songs (BMI). All rights reserved.
International Copyright Secured. Used by permission.

Bb Instrument

Near You

Francis Craig/Kermit Goell

Tenor Sax
(or Bb Trumpet)

©Warner Bros. Inc. (ASCAP). All rights reserved.
International Copyright Secured. Used by permission.

B♭ Instrument

Green, Green Grass of Home

Claude Putnam, Jr.

Tenor Sax
(or B♭ Trumpet)

©Sony ATV Songs (BMI). All rights reserved.
International Copyright Secured. Used by permission.

Good Hearted Woman

Waylon Jennings/Willie Nelson

©Polygram Intl (BMI)/Full Nelson Music Inc. (BMI). All rights reserved.
International Copyright Secured. Used by permission.

Busted

Harlan Howard

©Sony ATV Songs (BMI). All rights reserved.
International Copyright Secured. Used by permission.

Well I am no thief but a man can go wrong when he's bus-ted The

food that we canned last sum-mer is gone and I'm bus-ted Well the

fields are all bare and the cot-ton won't grow Me and my fam-ly's got to pack up and go but I

wan-na make a liv-ing, just where I don't know cause I'm bus-ted

D 9 *Ad libs until fade*

B♭ Instrument

Java

Schack/Friday/Tyler/Toussaint

Tenor Sax
(or B♭ Trumpet)

©Toseland Music Publishing Inc. (BMI). All rights reserved.
International Copyright Secured. Used by permission.

Nine to Five

Dolly Parton

©Velvet Apple Music (BMI)/Warner Tamerlane Publishing (BMI). All rights reserved.
International Copyright Secured. Used by permission.

B♭ Instrument

Pretty Woman

Roy Orbison/Joe Melson/Ray Bush

Tenor Sax
(or B♭ Trumpet)

©Acuff Rose Music/Orbi Lee Music/Barbara Orbison Music (BMI). All rights reserved.
International Copyright Secured. Used by permission.

Yakety Sax

Randolph/Rich

© Sony ATV Songs (BMI). All rights reserved.
International Copyright Secured. Used by permission.

Crazy

Willie Nelson

©Sony/ATV Songs (BMI). All rights reserved.
International Copyright Secured. Used by permission.

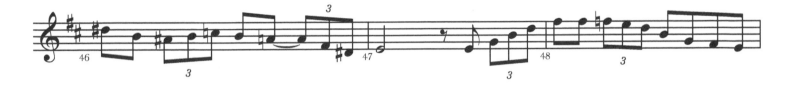

E♭ Instrument

You Don't Know Me

Eddy Arnold/Cindy Walker

©Unichappel Music Inc. (BMI). All rights reserved.
International Copyright Secured. Used by permission.

Last Date

One measure of taps precedes music

Floyd Cramer

Eb Alto Sax

©Acuff Rose Music Inc. (BMI). All rights reserved.
International Copyright Secured. Used by permission.

Night Life

Breeland/Nelson/Buskirk

E♭ Alto Sax

©Glad Music (BMI)/Sony ATV Songs (BMI). All rights reserved.
International Copyright Secured. Used by permission.

Near You

Francis Craig/Kermit Goell

©Warner Bros. Inc. (ASCAP). All rights reserved.
International Copyright Secured. Used by permission.

Green, Green Grass of Home

Claude Putnam Jr.

©Sony ATV Songs (BMI). All rights reserved.
International Copyright Secured. Used by permission.

Eb Instrument

Good Hearted Woman

Waylon Jennings/Willie Nelson

Eb Alto Sax

©Polygram Intl (BMI)/Full Nelson Music Inc. (BMI). All rights reserved.
International Copyright Secured. Used by permission.

E♭ Instrument

Busted

Harlan Howard

E♭ Alto Sax

©Sony ATV Songs (BMI). All rights reserved.
International Copyright Secured. Used by permission.

E♭ Instrument

Well I am no thief but a man can go wrong when he's bus-ted The

food that we canned last sum-mer is gone and I'm bus-ted Well the

fields are all bare and the cot-ton won't grow Me and my fam-ly's got to pack up and go but I

wan-na make a liv-ing, just where I don't know cause I'm bus-ted

D9 *Ad libs until fade*

Java

Schack/Friday/Tyler/Toussaint

©Toseland Music Publishing Inc. (BMI). All rights reserved.
International Copyright Secured. Used by permission.

Nine to Five

Dolly Parton

©Velvet Apple Music (BMI)/Warner Tamerlane Publishing (BMI). All rights reserved.
International Copyright Secured. Used by permission.

Eb Instrument

Pretty Woman

Roy Orbison/Joe Melson/Ray Bush

©Acuff Rose Music/Orbi Lee Music/Barbara Orbison Music (BMI). All rights reserved.
International Copyright Secured. Used by permission.

Yakety Sax

Randolph/Rich

©Sony ATV Songs (BMI). All rights reserved.
International Copyright Secured. Used by permission.

D.C. al Coda
repeat good on D.C.

⊕ *coda*

MORE GREAT GUITAR PUBLICATIONS FROM

Music Minus One

**Luigi Boccherini –
Guitar Quintet in
D Major No. 4,
"Fandango"**
*Performed by the Da Vinci
Quartet*
Book/CD Pack
00400062......................$14.99

**Max Bruch –
Concerto No. 1 for
Electric Guitar & Orchestra**
*Performed by Theron Welch
Accompaniment: Stuttgart
Symphony Orchestra*
Book/CD Pack
00400124......................$14.99

**Ferdinando Carulli –
Guitar Concertos**
**E Minor, Op. 140
A Major, Op. 8A**
*Performed by Christian
Reichert
Accompaniment: Rousse
Philharmonic Orchestra*
Book/Online Audio
00400641......................$16.99

**Mario Castelnuovo-
Tedesco – Guitar
Concerto in D Major, Op. 99**
*Performed by Christian
Reichert
Accompaniment: Plovdiv
Philharmonic Orchestra*
Book/Online Audio
00400683......................$16.99

**Mauro Giuliani –
Guitar Concerto
No. 1 in A Major, Op. 30**
*Performed by Christian
Reichert
Accompaniment: Plovdiv
Philharmonic Orchestra*
Book/Online Audio
00400065......................$19.99

**Manuel Ponce –
Concierto del Sur**
*Performed by Christian
Reichert
Accompaniment: Plovdiv
Symphony Orchestra*
Book/2-CD Pack
00400114....................$19.99

**Joaquin Rodrigo –
Fantasía para un
Gentilhombre**
*Performed by Christian
Reichert
Accompaniment: Plovdiv
Philharmonic Orchestra*
Downloadable Edition
01006793....................$34.99

**Fernando Sor –
Classic Guitar Duos**
*Performed by Christian
Reichert, primo guitar and
Beata Bedkowska-Huang,
secondo guitar*
Book/2-CD Pack
00400068....................$19.99

**Antonio Vivaldi –
Two Concerto for
Guitar and Orchestra**
**C Major, RV 425
D Major, RV 93**
*Performed by Christian
Reichert
Accompaniment: Taunus
String Orchestra*
Book/Online Audio
00400067 ....$19.99

**Orchestra Gems for
Classical Guitar**
*Performed by Andrew
LaFreniere
Accompaniment: Stuttgart
Festival Orchestra*
Book/CD Pack
00400064....................$14.99

GUITAR & FLUTE DUETS

**Mario Castelnuovo-
Tedesco – Sonatina
Op. 205 & Mauro Giuliani
– Serenata, Op. 127**
*Performed by Christian
Reichert
Accompaniment: Katarzyna
Bury, flute*
Book/2-CD Pack
00400688 ....$19.99

**Astor Piazzolla –
Histoire du Tango &
Other Latin Classics**
*Performed by Christian
Reichert
Accompaniment: Katarzyna
Bury, flute*
Book/Online Audio
00400066 ....$24.99

**Bossa, Samba &
Tango Duets**
**For Guitar and Flute
Plus Percussion**
*Performed by Christian
Reichert
Accompaniment: Katarzyna
Bury, flute*
Book/Online Audio
00400719 ....$14.99

**Guitar & Flute
Duets – Volume 1**
*Performed by Edward Flower
Accompaniment: Jeremy
Barlow, flute*
Book/2-CD Pack
00400063 ....$19.99

To see a full listing of
Music Minus One publications, visit
halleonard.com/MusicMinusOne

Music Minus One
HAL•LEONARD®
Prices, contents, and availability subject
to change without notice.